Struggling
To Be Me

Struggling To Be Me

No Longer Silent and Invisible At The Table

LETTIE AR–RAHMAAN

ARPress
ILLUMINATING IDEAS
EMPOWERING VOICES

ARPress
45 Dan Road Suite 5
Canton MA 02021

Hotline: 1(888) 821-0229
Fax: 1(508) 545-7580

Ordering Information:
Quantity sales. Special discounts are available on quantity purchases by corporations, associations, and others. For details, contact the publisher at the address above.

Printed in the United States of America.

ISBN-13:	Softcover	979-8-89676-511-0
	eBook	979-8-89676-512-7

Library of Congress Control Number: 2024924547

Table of Contents

Invitation

I'm Willetta Ar-Rahmaan.

Yes, it's different from the name printed on the cover. As a child, I was called "Lettie," and I love it. Of course, people also know me by my government name. Yet, Lettie is the voice I've grown into, and I've grown to love Lettie.

I've been shifting gears for a long time. Shifting came out of my struggle with gender, cultural, racial and educational discrimination. As I reflected on my life's last 40 plus years, it appears that I struggled early and often. During my battles, I learned to drive a stick-shift vehicle called a 5-speed or manual transmission vehicle. Learning to drive a stick shift wasn't easy. You have to manage the clutch, gas pedal, brake, and gearshift while keeping your eyes on the road.

When I think about my struggles, the first vivid image resonates with me is learning to drive a stick shift at 18 years old. My best friend and our boyfriends were in Oxford, North Carolina. It was a gray Toyota Celica Supra. My boyfriend asked me if I wanted to learn to drive a stick. I enthusiastically said, "Yes," while thinking I would do so once we arrived back in Durham, North Carolina. To my surprise, he pulled the car over to the side of the road. We were on top of a hill when he said, "Now get us off this hill." I don't know how long it took me to get off that hill. However, by the time we got back to Durham, I was shifting gears like a pro. If you haven't driven a stick shift be aware, getting off a hill is a struggle. As I reflect on that day and all the days of my life, becoming Lettie has been a struggle.

This book will walk you through a portion of my childhood years as I pressed into adulthood. Our formative years shape our lives in negative and positive ways. Each area of my life has had challenges and support. In the beauty of it all, my strength came through holding the God of my Ancestors' hand, the nudging of the Holy Ghost, and holding on to Psalms 59, 86, and 112.

These Psalms ministered to my mind, spirit and soul when I wasn't aware of the danger around me. Over the past 30 years, I've reflected on these Psalms. They brought me comfort, peace and assurance of God's presence and my Ancestors. As you read them, may you experience the same.

Psalm 59

Prayer for Deliverance from Enemies

To the leader: Do Not Destroy. Of David. A Miktam, when Saul ordered his house to be watched in order to kill him.

[1]Deliver me from my enemies, O my God; protect me from those who rise up against me. [2] Deliver me from those who work evil; from the bloodthirsty save me. [3]Even now they lie in wait for my life; the mighty stir up strife against me. For no transgression or sin of mine, O Lord, [4]for no fault of mine, they run and make ready. Rouse yourself, come to my help and see! [5]You, Lord God of hosts, are God of Israel. Awake to punish all the nations; spare none of those who treacherously plot evil.

Selah

⁶Each evening they come back, howling like dogs and prowling about the city. ⁷There they are, bellowing with their mouths, with sharp words on their lips— for "Who," they think, "will hear us?"⁸ But you laugh at them, O Lord; you hold all the nations in derision. ⁹O my strength; I will watch for you; for you, O God, are my fortress. ¹⁰My God in his steadfast love will meet me; my God will let me look in triumph on my enemies. ¹¹Do not kill them, or my people may forget; make them totter by your power, and bring them down, O Lord, our shield. ¹²For the sin of their mouths, the words of their lips, let them be trapped in their pride. For the cursing and lies that they utter, ¹³consume them in wrath; consume them until they are no more. Then it will be known to the ends of the earth that God rules over Jacob.

Selah

¹⁴ Each evening they come back, howling like dogs and prowling about the city. ¹⁵They roam about for food and growl if they do not get their fill. ¹⁶But I will sing of your might; I will sing aloud of your steadfast love in the morning. For you have been a fortress for me and a refuge in the day of my distress. ¹⁷O my strength, I will sing praises to you, for you, O God, are my fortress, the God who shows me, steadfast love.

Psalm 86

Supplication for Help against Enemies

A Prayer of David.

¹Incline your ear, O Lord, and answer me, for I am poor and needy. ²Preserve my life, for I am devoted to you; save your servant who trusts in you. You are my God; ³be gracious to me, O Lord, for to you do I cry all day long. ⁴Gladden the soul of your servant, for to you, O Lord, I lift up my soul. ⁵For you, O Lord, are good and forgiving, abounding in steadfast love to all who call on you. ⁶Give ear, O Lord, to my prayer; listen to my cry of supplication. ⁷In the day of my trouble, I call on you, for you will answer me. ⁸There is none like you among the gods, O Lord, nor are there any works like yours. ⁹All the nations you have made

shall come and bow down before you, O Lord, and shall glorify your name. [10]For, you are great and do wondrous things; you alone are God. [11]Teach me your way, O Lord, that I may walk in your truth; give me an undivided heart to revere your name. [12]I give thanks to you, O Lord my God, with my whole heart, and I will glorify your name forever. [13]For great is your steadfast love toward me; you have delivered my soul from the depths of Sheol. [14]O God, the insolent rise up against me; a band of ruffians seeks my life, and they do not set you before them. [15]But you, O Lord, are a God merciful and gracious, slow to anger and abounding in steadfast love and faithfulness. [16]Turn to me and be gracious to me; give your strength to your servant; save the child of your serving girl. [17]Show me a sign of your favor, so that those who hate me may see it and be put to shame, because you, Lord, have helped me and comforted me.

Psalm 112

Blessings of the Righteous

[1]Praise the Lord! Happy are those who fear the Lord, who greatly delights in his commandments. [2]Their descendants will be mighty in the land; the generation of the upright will be blessed. [3]Wealth and riches are in their houses, and their righteousness endures forever. [4]They rise in the darkness as a light for the upright; they are gracious, merciful, and righteous. [5]It is well with those who deal generously and lend, who conduct their affairs with justice. [6]For the righteous will never be moved; they will be remembered forever. [7]They are not afraid of evil tidings; their hearts are firm, secure in the Lord. [8]Their hearts are steady; they will not be afraid; in the end, they will look in triumph on their foes. [9]They have distributed freely; they have given to the poor; their righteousness endures forever; their horn is exalted in honor. [10]The wicked see it and are angry; they gnash their teeth and melt away; the desire of the wicked comes to nothing.

My seminary journey opened my eyes to the context of these Psalms. There was a perspective in life I didn't see until I wrestled with the biblical culture. The biblical culture is God's redemption work in the larger society. As I examined these three psalms, I recognized the struggle between society and humanity during biblical times hadn't changed a lot today. There were women leaders throughout biblical times. The view of these women has been through the hierarchal and patriarchal lenses of society. Society norms changed, especially during COVID-19. COVID-19 has caused the entire world to stop, struggle and survive as a global community.

I now see how God uniquely held me for such a time like this. What is a time like this? It's the rise and struggle of women leaders, who are now heard and seen at the table in male-dominated careers!

Sitting in Neutral

I was born Willetta Jean Bracey in New Haven, Connecticut. Surprise! The shifting started early. I was born with a congenital disability that resulted in my undergoing surgery, before the age of three, to repair a hole in my heart vessel. I grew up in the Nation of Islam (NOI). My parents converted from Christianity to Islam before my birth. My father was the chef at Yale-New Haven Hospital, and a minister in Islam. My mother was a stay-at-home mother and became a certified nursing assistant (CNA) later. My first memory of struggling was my parents' carefulness when I wanted to be active in sports. They worried how the strenuous activity would affect the repaired heart vessel. I didn't pay much attention to their concerns, as I wasn't fully aware of the circumstances of my birth and the surgery until I reached junior high school.

During my academic years, I encountered the biggest struggle of my young life. Until second or third grade, I attended Hamden Public School. That was the same year my parents transferred my siblings and me to Sis. Clara Muhammad School in New Haven. They wanted us to be educated in Islam and felt it was a better move for us. I didn't notice the change right away, but saw my childhood friends only on weekends.

I didn't sense the shift until one day, I realized my brother went to school in the morning, and my younger sisters and I went during the afternoon. It was odd, but I didn't question it. In the Nation of Islam (NOI), I soon discovered the treatment of boys and girls was different. In public gatherings, men and boys (boys who were weaned and old enough) sat on one side, and the women and girls sat on another side. That was certainly different from anything I had ever experienced. We wore uniforms to school and the temple. Girls and women covered their heads with a scarf.

One day I wanted to climb the tree in our backyard. I not only climbed the tree, but I also put on my brother's jeans and climbed the tree. You would have thought that I committed a crime. My mother scolded me because girls are forbidden to wear any pants without a long blouse, jacket, or dress to cover their hips, buttocks, and thighs in Islam. I was a skinny girl. My brother called me "Lettie Spaghetti." It was then that I became aware of gender discrimination and resistance directed towards me. It was present all the time, but I gradually woke to gender discrimination at nine years old. From that moment, I challenged my parents' decisions on gender separation, clothing, and more. Every day, all day, it seemed everything I heard revolved around what girls couldn't do. There was a lack of discussion around girls' roles outside of domestic work, administrative assistant, teacher, or a nurse. Ironically, during this time, Ella T. Grasso, Connecticut's governor, was the first woman leader I didn't see in the traditional "woman" role.

Growing up, I often competed with my brother. He loved to draw, and I would do the same. He would disassemble electronics, and I would reassemble them. I was that older sister. I was that girl who enjoyed puzzles, patterns, and pictures. As my eyes witnessed gender discrimination, my mind didn't understand. I never said much about my love of science and electronics; I kept it to myself.

The last two years of elementary school were odd. We returned to Hamden Public School. I was interested in cheerleading. I knew all the cheers, but my parents didn't allow me to participate since the skirts were too short. Once again, the NOI and my parents maintained girls' dress protocol. In Islam, girls always wore a long dress with pants. At the time,

I didn't understand the reasons behind these rules. I just followed the rules. I now understand that the rules were about protecting my body from unwanted sexual advances. If I dressed as undesirable, I would not tempt men or boys. The message I received was that I couldn't be seen as attractive or pretty.

The last year of elementary school was exciting, especially the music class. The teacher asked us what instruments we wanted to play. My first and only choice was the drums. I loved music. My older sisters would play records that had great percussions. The beat of the percussions spoke to my soul. As I reached for the drumsticks and pad, my teacher told me that the drums were for the boys. She gave me the French horn. I was devastated! She asked me what I wanted to play, but then she denied my request. Therefore, someone gave me what they thought I should receive. It didn't make sense to me. As a form of resistance and rebellion, I didn't learn to read music or play the French horn. I carried that instrument around for a year without playing it because it wasn't what I wanted.

Elementary school and those formative years opened my eyes to the ways women showed resistance and discrimination towards girls. During these formative years, girls mostly saw more women teachers than men. Some women passed down to their daughters and granddaughters gender roles depending on their own viewpoints on those roles. In elementary school, girls start to notice their strengths and weaknesses. I was always the shy one. I didn't use my voice because I was taught that children are to be seen and not heard and that girls shouldn't demonstrate being more knowledgeable than boys. Most of the time, I knew more than others, but I remained silent because of my upbringing. Therefore, when people told me no, I internalized it as a personal attack because that's all I knew at that time. At the end of my elementary school years, Willetta Bracey disappeared, and Willetta Ar-Rahmaan appeared.

Gear 1: In a New World

I was 11 years old at the start of seventh grade, and I have a new last name, "Ar-Rahmaan." It means merciful in Arabic. Changing our last name removed the stigma of slavery and the given slave master's name. This new name singled me out more. My parents carefully selected this name, and they were proud of our new chosen name. From time to time, people continued to call us by our former last name. I started a new chapter that included a new school, a unique name, and little freedom. I always loved music, but I wouldn't touch an instrument. I just sang in the school chorus and listened to music at home. My parents rarely bought 45s or albums. They listened to the radio. We listened to AM Gold until I discovered the FM station.

Here's a story that reflects my curiosity as a child. I grew up with a big antenna on the roof and a UHF/VHF switcher in the house. Before my oldest sister moved out of the home, she had a stereo system in her room. We lived in a three-story detached garage home. Her room was on the third floor, which was the attic. When she hung her antenna out the window, she could pick up the radio station, WBLS, in New York City. However, my parents' stereo system couldn't pick it up downstairs in the den. Curiosity got the best of me. The engineering spirit in me removed the antenna from the stereo, stripped the wire and connected it to the

UHF/VHF switcher. I found WBLS, and it was just as clear as it was on the third floor. No one asked how it connected, but they enjoyed it.

During 7th grade and part of 8th grade at Hamden Public School, I discovered new interests in diving, photography, and competing with my brother again. This time, he played basketball and baseball, and I wanted to play basketball. My parents allowed me to play sports and wear shorts and a T-shirt. I felt I had arrived. I played basketball as a center in both seventh and eighth grades. We had two coaches, a man and a woman. The coaches and team provided balance, but I didn't feel that my parents supported me as they supported my brother. My parents rarely attended my weekday games and practices because their work schedules conflicted with our games' times. They attended my brother's games on Saturdays. I brushed it off at the time, but little did I know, this lack of support would continually resurface in my friendships and relationships.

I was excited about junior high. I enjoyed home economics class, history and math. As the oldest daughter in the home, I was expected to prepare meals and the automatic built-in babysitter. The skills that I learned in home economics were not new to me. I was already cooking, sewing, cleaning and doing other household chores. I watched my dad prepare meals, but on Saturday mornings, we had chores to do with clean-up music playing before we could watch cartoons and *Soul Train.*

When I learned to cook new meals in school, my parents were invited to eat with us. Again, their work schedules prevented them from attending. However, my teachers encouraged me. My father especially encouraged me more when I cooked those same meals at home by helping me season the food.

Being the oldest girl at home, I had to prep dinner, get my siblings off the school bus and do my homework. Life was awkward as I sought to balance my responsibilities and extracurricular activities. Still I didn't show much interest in science and electronics, but I discovered theatre and photography. During the summer after seventh grade, I participated in the local junior high school tutoring program three blocks away from home. I quickly discovered a drama class. I worked backstage, made props and occasionally played an understudy for nonspeaking roles. Until the night of the production, I shared the play, invitation, and role

I played with my family. However, I wasn't able to see the performance. My parents were concerned about my safety since the performance began at 8:30 p.m. All I wanted to do was honor my word. The response was "No," even after advocating for myself. Once again, I was silenced and let down for something I deeply wanted to do.

In the middle of eighth grade, my parents announced, "We are moving." My mother, younger siblings, and nieces, moved to the South in January 1980. When I declared that I wanted to remain with my father in Connecticut, my parents agreed. It wasn't easy living in that big house without the rest of my family. My victory did not last for long as a few incidents happened. One day my cousin and his best friend, "my boyfriend," skipped school, came to my school and tried to get me out of class. I wasn't aware of this until I was called to the principal's office. The principal interrogated me about their visit. I didn't have answers, and my father was informed of the incident. Therefore, a few weeks later, my father said we were going to Durham, North Carolina. On that particular Friday morning, my father told me to clean out my locker and let the school know I'm withdrawing. I didn't do it because it didn't make sense to me. After school that day, my father informed me I was going to live with my mother. I was angry, and I tried to advocate for myself. No matter how much I yelled, cried and ran away to my second oldest sister's place, I was leaving Hamden, Connecticut. At this point, I refused to pack anything; I was snippy and angry. On that third Friday night in April 1980, my father drove me to Durham. I didn't speak to him for the entire trip. Two months before the eighth-grade school year ended, my world turned upside down. I didn't bid my farewell to friends, clean out my locker or talk to my boyfriend. I felt abandoned and rejected. I was in a new place, a new school, and a new way of life.

Gear 2: Hope Disappeared

L ife had changed forever. It would be two years before I saw any of my Connecticut family or friends again. Much had changed in those two years. I was a single teenage mother of a daughter, and we lived in a housing project. That once vibrant girl who loved sports, music, cooking, photography, science, theatre and engineering disappeared.

I didn't fit into this new space. People called me ugly and conceited. I lost my vision of the future and my voice. The seven years I spent in North Carolina weren't easy. When my mother enrolled me in school as an eighth-grader, school administrators told her that I needed to be in the seventh grade because of my age. After much debate, I remained in the eighth grade to finish the school year. School released in early June. I only knew a few people in the neighborhood that summer. Therefore, I ended up with the wrong crowd. I rebelled because I wanted to be back in Connecticut. Eventually, I realized North Carolina was my new home and that I could not leave any time soon. I gave up on my life and my dreams. My voice was silenced.

At the start of the ninth grade, we moved from one side of Durham to Northern Durham County into the housing projects; Oxford Manor, also called Braggtown. This place was hell. I experienced additional sexual abuse, manipulation and a constant need to prove my toughness. That meant constantly fighting someone.

Upon arriving at the housing projects, I experienced a brief honeymoon period. As the new girl in the neighborhood, people had lots of questions for me. They wanted to know where I had moved from, my interests and whether I supported Duke or Carolina basketball. When I said that I was from Connecticut, they usually responded, "I didn't know Black people lived there." My basketball choice was the University of Connecticut (UCONN) Huskies all the way. Life dramatically changed for me as a ninth-grader. As the oldest girl in the house, I needed to be in the same school district as my siblings. To accommodate my mother's work schedule, I was pushed back to junior high for my ninth-grade year instead of remaining in high school as a freshman

I struggled with making friends, tried out for the basketball team, and enjoyed shop class. But then my entire life crashed. Shortly before my 14th birthday, my family and I discovered that I was pregnant. Immediately, I lost hope. Everyone believed that I was just another statistic—a baby having a baby. I felt alone when I went to my doctor's appointments by myself. I felt alone when I enrolled in a school for pregnant girls. I felt alone as I stayed indoors throughout my pregnancy. I felt alone as I dealt with my emotions, depression, and complicated life. I was isolated from everyone except those who lived in our home. My pregnancy was high risk because of my repaired congenital disability. People saw me as damaged goods. My mother's friends gossiped about me. I was ashamed. As I walked to the bus stop for school, I would walk with my head down. I heard people whisper about my pregnancy. I saw their disappointment with me. The school for pregnant girls provided basic ninth-grade education. We learned what to expect during labor and how to care for babies. No one expected anything spectacular to happen in my life. I, too, had no expectations for myself. I even contemplated death by suicide. Because of this, I lost the ability to speak up for myself. My voice was now muted.

When it was time to give birth, one of the nurses in the labor and delivery room commented, "She will be back." Little did she know that I didn't plan any more pregnancies because I planned my life to be childless. The women in my life didn't prepare me for motherhood. We didn't have conversations about the birds and the bees. We had a sex education class at school. The class didn't include information about sexual abuse. I sensed I disappointed my family. They didn't know how to help me deal with the trauma I experienced. I went from childhood to adulthood in one year.

After the birth of my daughter, my father said to me, "Don't have any more children until you are married." No one encouraged me to dream. Instead, they taught me how to care for a house, marry a good man and have more children. My life choices were limited to add to my misery. I experienced racial discrimination attending my first and last football game, as I was called out of my name. My character was attacked, especially by those who didn't know me. I had hate, anger and rage bottled up inside of me. I lost interest in life, I felt shame, and I was embarrassed. Years later, I understood that I had suffered from postpartum depression. I was angry at the world. I didn't have much-needed support, and I no longer trusted people, including family. I accepted the motto: What happens in the house stays in the house. What happens outside of the house is ignored.

Gear 3: A Spark of Hope

This girl with big dreams couldn't dream anymore. I no longer dreamed of playing basketball, becoming a photographer or an engineer. I was angry all the time, and I didn't care about life. I resented people who appeared to have a normal childhood and high school experience.

I started my 10th-grade year with a 4-month-old baby. I struggled. Again, I was an outsider navigating life without a clear direction or path. I wasn't prepared academically to move into the 10th grade. I was behind in math as the school I attended while pregnant wasn't equipped for some of the classes I needed. I had lost focus and concentration.

Discouraged, I didn't work to my full potential. I failed geometry. Basically, I lost interest in school. All I wanted was out.

I was left to navigate and figure out life on my own. I was tired and overwhelmed as a teenage mother. I didn't ask for help, and no one offered assistance, so I struggled for class daily. It showed up in my schoolwork. I rarely prepared my homework. I would do it on the school bus or right before class. People didn't expect much of me, and I didn't do much to change their minds. Towards the end of 10th grade, I chose the business curriculum for graduation. I heard that my peers who took office occupation class were able to leave school early. Well, that wasn't an option for me, so I took the Directed Office Occupation (DOO) class. I learned to type, organize, and file. I enrolled in accounting classes. As I became proficient in typing, I started offering my services for typing term papers. Although I didn't say much about my interests, my parents purchased an electric typewriter to practice my typing at home. I created my first job and became an entrepreneur. I enjoyed typing and being responsible, but I continued to work below my potential. I didn't prepare adequately for school assignments or tests.

In the DOO class, I typed syllabi, exams, quizzes and letters for teachers. I learned to proofread. There was a level of confidentiality and responsibility needed. Ironically, when I was in elementary school, I was called to the office to help answer phones and use the public announcement system. These responsibilities sparked my independence and confidence. I wasn't excited about high school, but I was excited to assist others. I became bored with school and life.

I feared dropping out of high school. I thought about the military and took the Military Aptitude Test. I scored in the 90th percentile on the electronic and mechanical portions of the test. The results did not surprise me. The military pursued me, but I wasn't interested. However, the score surprised my guidance counselor. She reviewed my school performance and was amazed to see that I had been a high-performing student before moving to North Carolina. She tried to intervene and find out what was going on with me. At this point, I didn't trust anyone. I didn't talk about my life's trauma, and I felt that everyone had written me off.

My counselor talked to me about the North Carolina School of Science and Mathematics. I was interested, but attending meant I would have to move away from home. I tried to talk my mom into letting me go there since the school was just across town. My mother did not budge because I would be away from home and away from my 18-month-old daughter and siblings. My mother depended on me heavily since my father never moved to North Carolina, and my older siblings had their own families. At that point, I lost hope things would change for me.

One day a computer showed up in an accounting class. I loved accounting, and it showed in my work. It was a Tandy 1000 with a 5 1/4 floppy disk. My accounting teacher walked us through the software. I was so intrigued that I asked if I could learn more during study hall. Instantly, I became a tutor for the accounting software. I took pride in teaching others how to navigate this new computer and software. As a Black teenage mother on the verge of quitting high school as a senior, I was hopeful. There was a woman who saw my capability and helped nurture the soft skill of tutoring.

However, my time as an unofficial teacher's assistant was short-lived due to envy and jealousy. I attended a majority-white high school, where most Black students were bused in from public housing, rural areas, and subdivisions. From the 10th to the 12th grade, I endured countless mean black girls. Behind my back, they called me names and then smiled in my face. I kept to myself and felt comfortable with my white friends because we learned from each other. I recognized during high school that I loved to collaborate, teach and tutor. I was good at it, but some thought that I was too confident. I certainly didn't think that I was too confident. I carried myself with respect, and I held my head up. As graduation approached, I tried to be like a raincoat—letting things roll off me.

My accounting teacher tried to be fair in allotting us computer time. During group assignments, there would be three or four people around the computer. One of the mean black girls in the class told the teacher that there were three white students and one black student in our group. The black girl considered me as a white girl. Mind you, this comment came from the same Black girl who struggled with the new technology. As I look back on that situation, I now realize her behavior was calling out for help. It's easy for people to destroy our character instead of asking for help. I would have helped her if she had asked. Her followers encouraged her to keep insulting me. I can't say whether she was trying to be funny, cause harm, or make me angry. However, her actions pushed the teacher to stop group assignments and to stop me from assisting others.

Ironically, later in the school year, those in the mean girl's crew sought me out for computer assistance. Instead of asking for help and acknowledging one's skills, people often resort to jealousy. Unfortunately, since that high school incident, I've encountered other women's resistance. I've worked in areas to cultivate my skills and asked questions when things didn't make sense. When I try to show other women what I've learned, some were thankful, and some were not. I'm wired to easily see the patterns and puzzles pieces of software and scenarios.

At my high school, most girls didn't help each other; instead, they competed with one another. I didn't care about outshining, insulting or being envious—I just wanted to help others where they struggled. High school was rough, but I made it. I didn't take any computer classes, but at home, I read a book on BASIC.

Interestingly, I went through 12 years of education in two states, only to now realize that I had a handful of women and two male teachers who encouraged me. However, it was during my secondary schooling that I experienced more misogyny and racism in the South, from both girls and women, regardless of their ethnicity. The DOO classes in high school helped me see myself differently during my struggles. I learned to work independently and take pride in my work. I had to fight with words to graduate and to receive my high school diploma. That's because of Ms. Shirl Wilson, an English teacher, who tried to block me from graduating. I struggled in English and by the time I got to her class, I lost interest. One day I went to her classroom to talk about my grade for graduation. She wouldn't budge. Admittedly, I could have done better, but I was tired and overwhelmed.

Here's what led to my discussion with Ms. Wilson. Just a month before graduation, my daughters' father was killed. I received the news on a Saturday night after getting off work. It took me a few days to return to school. My teachers were sympathetic, and those who knew my situation were as well. When I got to the accounting class, I encountered the same mean black girl previously mentioned. This time, I guess she was trying to be funny, but I wasn't in the mood. She screamed, "You don't know who your daughter's father is." She then laughed. Filled with grief and anger, I picked up my duffle bag filled with books and prepared to throw the bag at her when my best friend, Donna, stopped my arm in motion. At that time, the mean girl realized I had enough. I was suspended for ten days, and she spread a rumor that I cheated on my exam. I did not need to cheat because I had a B+ average in the class.

Therefore, the discussion a day before graduation with Ms. Wilson provided me with the grace I needed. She told me, "If you don't get a handle on your anger, you won't make it in this world!" I passed her class with a D and walked across the stage the next day. I now see the wisdom in Ms. Wilson's words to me.

I didn't enroll in a four-year college. I stayed home and attended a community college. 1984 was a rough year. A week after my 18th birthday, my father died. It was six months after my daughter's father's death. My father's death added to my anger. I grieved my father's death extremely hard. I was a daddy's girl, his oldest daughter. I was hurt, and there was nothing anyone could do. Therapy wasn't offered or even mentioned. We lived by the motto "what happened in the house stays in the house." We buried my father during Thanksgiving week of 1984. I lost my way for a while. I didn't have the energy to pursue education, go to work or talk to anyone. I didn't have any positive coping skills. I became reckless about life until my brother gave me a message.

Following my father's death, my brother had a dream in which my father appeared and left instructions for me to read Psalms 59, 86 and 112. I pressed my brother for more information, but he couldn't tell me anything more than those three psalms. A Bible was rare in our home, but I found a small New Testament with the Psalms in the King James Version Bible translation, which I didn't understand.

I read those Psalms daily. I kept the small testament in the driver's side pocket of my car. There were three emerging themes in these psalms. They were deliverance, protection and faithfulness. I was still angry with God even after reading these scriptures. I blamed God for my father's death, the move to North Carolina and the sexual abuse against me. By this time, I avoided all institutional religion and stepped into a church only twice—for a funeral and a wedding.

Gear 4: Waking up my Gifts

I n the Summer of 1985, I went back to community college and majored in Data Processing. Ironically, my mother majored in the same curriculum while I was in high school. She struggled with it and dropped it after a year. I stuck with it for two years but did not complete the program. I worked odd jobs, cared for my daughter and tried several times to get into IBM in Research Triangle Park, North Carolina (RTP). I was unsuccessful, but I didn't give up. Because of my community college education and training in electronic manufacturing, I received two great opportunities. Looking back, I now understand that 1986 was a transformative year. I didn't reflect on discrimination of any sort. I started mapping a path to succeed in community college. I learned how to strategize, lprocesses quickly and think critically. I had what I needed to succeed in a male-dominated career field confidently.

In the spring of 1987, my childhood boyfriend and I eloped. I turned down an entry-level developer's job at Honeywell because my focus was electronic manufacturing. By mid-summer, my daughter, my husband and I went home to Connecticut to visit. On our return trip, our vehicle experienced mechanical issues and broke down on the Jersey Turnpike, forcing us to go back to New Haven, Connecticut. Once the vehicle was repaired, we returned to North Carolina to retrieve items from our apartment as we had decided to move back to Connecticut.

My mother and younger siblings had moved back to Connecticut a year earlier.

The first year back in Connecticut was hard. I struggled to land a decent job even with the soldering skills I had acquired in electronic manufacturing. However, within a year, I secured a data entry job at a millwork company. While working at the millwork company, I enrolled in the local community college and started my Associate Degree in Data Processing at South Central Community College.

I found my footing. But little did I know working in corporate America would be challenging. Before graduation, I accepted a temporary assignment as a junior executive administrative assistant for IBM. I enhanced my organizational skills, became proficient with office tools, and unleashed creativity. I also learned how to use a tool called PROFS, an HTML-based system for creating presentation slides and learned how to create label templates using a word processor. As a contractor, I put my best foot forward while working with professional women and men. I was pleasant and respectable. Yet, some people were still rude. However, I didn't allow their rudeness to distract me from doing my job.

Contracting assignments were limited to 18 months, but I was given an extension for a few extra months to work with databases. During those 22 months, I graduated with my associate degree and transferred to a four-year college as a junior in the business school as a computer science major. I was the first person in my immediate family to graduate from college.

When my contract ended, I struggled to find employment while attending school full-time. The job market was bleak. I worked at two part-time jobs in the data entry field and as an office manager until I landed a summer IT internship at Pratt & Whitney.

After the internship was over, I was on the job hunt again. The struggle of marriage, unresolved trauma, and the inability to find a job caused me to leave the place I loved. I went to Durham, North Carolina, to pick my daughter up from her summer vacation. I had plans to go to Ft. Hood, Texas, but I had to use all of my money to repair my broken vehicle. Reluctantly I stayed in Durham and started rebuilding my life as a divorced woman with a tween daughter.

Returning to North Carolina was bittersweet. It seemed that my past regarding racism, gender discrimination and other people's opinions of what I should do reared its ugly head. My struggles continued in Durham. My stubbornness, impatience and pride got the best of me. I quickly landed an administrative assistant position. Still, I refused to ask for help and had a hard time accepting help because people kept telling me what I needed to do. The temporary job ended, and my vehicle was repossessed, but my daughter and I had a roof over our heads. It took me almost six months to secure a full-time job. I had a two-year academic degree, administrative assistant skills and tech skills, but I did not have personal transportation. We survived on unemployment and Social Security benefits. We had enough for rent, bus fare and food. I didn't qualify for food stamps because my income was $5 more than the income guidelines.

In late spring, new transportation service from Durham to Raleigh was available. I was able to secure employment through a contract company. I landed back at IBM as an administrative assistant in the mobile and PC company. After working for almost 18 months, I enrolled in North Carolina Central University (NCCU) as a Computer Science major in the Business School. After a semester, I changed my degree major to study Computer Science in the Mathematics Department. I really wanted to attend North Carolina State's engineering program. I had to release that dream and stay local while my daughter was in middle school.

A year later, I felt it was time to move from an administrative role to a technical role. When I spoke to my manager at the contracting company about the position, she told me those roles were hard acquire and were typically for men. I was disappointed because of my credentials and my status as a full-time computer science major while working qualified me for the job. Perhaps my woman supervisor did not want me to get the job because she would be losing my exceptional skills as an executive administrative assistant. There were opportunities, but I ran into a traditional woman who didn't think I should be in a technical role.

What she didn't know was that I had just talked myself out of applying for the engineering program at North Carolina State University due to distance and raising a tween daughter.

This was the first time since high school that I had to deal with this kind of resistance. During those years, I worked odd jobs, retail jobs, including tech, data entry and administrative assistance jobs. Others encouraged me to grow my skills, learn as much as I could and be teachable. When resistance surfaced, I had to shift gears and create a plan. I wasn't taught how to handle conflict then. My coping skills were to ignore, stop talking and press forward. Therefore, I began working with the career planning and placement office at the university. Attending career fairs, modifying my resume and sharpening my interview skills were a top priority. When an opportunity matched my skills, the career office immediately notified me. During the 1994 Fall semester, I interviewed for a Junior System Engineer position at Northern Telecom (NORTEL). I received and accepted the offer. My new position started in January 1995.

Still, I kept trying to get into IBM again, but nothing materialized until September 1995, when I received a call for an interview as a co-op student. The internship at NORTEL lasted until December 1995. So, I accepted the offer from IBM and broke the news to my current co-op job.

In January 1996, I was an IBM co-op student, and my position turned into a long-term supplement employee. The girl who had stopped dreaming many years before began dreaming again. My life's goal was to work for IBM. Once I received access to the system, I sent two emails. The first was to Mrs. Celeste Bishop, my former neighbor in Hamden, Connecticut, and the second was to the former consultant manager, who responded, "You are not full-time." Her comment didn't bother me at all. I had a job, and I felt a weight lifted. I may not have been a full-time employee, but I finally got my foot in the door and on IBM's payroll rather than a consultant's payroll.

Today, as I reflect on my former manager and the situation, I think she didn't believe that I belonged in a tech position because I was a great Executive Adminstrative Assistant and people person. Her response triggered the same emotions that I experienced in elementary school when I grabbed the drumsticks and pad and was told it wasn't for me. I now know that some women and men will erect barriers in our career path based upon their own presuppositions. Some people believe that a woman who is a single mother is bad for their company's image and success. That was not the case with Doug Gzym, who took a chance on me. He took me under his wing and taught me how to take a computer apart, change out hard-drives, set up a LAN and plan the rollout of Lotus Notes for over 30 people.

As I continued my degree at NCCU, I worked up to 40 hours each week. My position changed from being a Co-Op Student to becoming a long-term supplemental employee. Mrs. Evelyn Watson was the manager of all the administrative assistants. Although I was not coding, I continued to repair computers, install software, and provide desk-side support in the Retail Store Solutions.

As I got closer to graduation, I needed to secure a full-time job. I interviewed with IBM and other corporations. I had no luck. Then, IBM flew me to Austin, Texas, despite my 2.5-grade point. I transferred in 100 credits from all of the colleges I attended. Working full time, raising a daughter and attending school full time affected my grades. If I had stayed in the business school, things would have been different. I struggled in the Mathematics Department. I was a COBOL developer. HTML came easy, but C++ and Pascal overwhelmed me and kicked my butt. I took classes that I didn't need, only to later discover that the curriculum had changed. However, I pushed through it.

With IBM experience, while in Austin, Texas, I thought I would immediately obtain a full-time job. One of the interviewers, a black man, told me that I wouldn't get a job at IBM because of my grade point average and that the best I could do was take a Helpdesk position he offered. He only focused on my grade point average rather than my entire resume and story. He could have at least provided advice that would help me prepare for the position. I rejected the interviewer's words and told him, "You don't know my story or what I went through to get here. All you see is what's on paper." I was so hurt.

I returned home from Austin, Texas, but I did not stop searching for a full-time job. I thought about the Helpdesk position in Charlotte, North Carolina, that was offered in Austin and compared it to my current long-term supplemental position. Charlotte's position paid less than my current position, and Charlotte's living cost was higher than Durham's. I talked to my manager Evelyn Watson. She told me that day, "You will not leave this position until you have a full-time job." With her help, we kept an eye open for opportunities.

A few months later, I interviewed in Charlotte as a college hire COBOL developer. Within weeks, I received a full-time offer from IBM for a new start-up organization called (ITRC) Insurance Technology Resource Center in Charlotte. I was converted to a full-time employee with no break in service. Mrs. Evelyn Watson saw me, my struggle and my tenacity. Also, she pulled me to the side, gave me some motherly and professional advice and then said, "No more colored jeans and add money to your 401K."

Moving to Charlotte brought about mixed emotions. I had to leave my home church, a loving faith community at Orange Grove Missionary Baptist Church.

My Christian journey began in Connecticut before returning to North Carolina. For a year, an IBM staff member in Connecticut kept inviting me to attend church services with his family. Ironically, the church was two blocks away from the home I grew up in Hamden, Connecticut. During my graduation year from NCCU, I converted to Christianity from Islam, and I accepted my ministry call. This call placed me in two male-dominated professions.

Gear 5: Clicking on all Cylinders

In 1998, I started a new full-time role with IBM in Charlotte, and I was licensed as a minister of the gospel later that year. Let me step back for a moment to 1991. That year, I attended Christian Tabernacle. I sensed a change in me, but I wasn't sure what it was.

Every Sunday around the dinner table, I would share the sermon that was preached and provide my thoughts about it. I did this for almost a year. During that time, everything turned upside down. I felt trapped and overwhelmed. Suddenly, I stopped attending church, but God wasn't finished with me. After moving to Durham, I did not participate in church again for a couple of years. In the summer of 1995, I felt the need to worship. My neighbor and I began visiting various churches. One Sunday, we went to a Holiness church. I didn't understand the difference between denominations. In Islam, there was one place for all to worship. During the worship service, the woman pastor asked for all visitors to come forward. We did so. She prayed with all of us. As we were returning to our seats, the pastor said, "You two ladies in the blue, please come back." We looked at each other and realized she was talking to us. Hesitantly and cautiously, we returned. She told my neighbor, "all you prayed about, God has worked it out." She turned to me and said, "God has work for you to do. Stop running." When service was over, we rushed out of the door, and that was the last time I stepped foot inside of a church for a long time.

This woman of God spoke words of encouragement, hope, and acceptance into my life. She didn't know that months earlier, I sat in my closet crying out to God, asking God to relieve me of my struggles because I was tired of struggling.

In 1996, I started attending Orange Grove Missionary Baptist Church under the pastoral leadership of Rev. Carl W. Kenney II. My neighbor went with me a few times, but I wouldn't go by myself. One day, my aunt called and told me that I had a cousin at NCCU. I connected with her, and once we connected, we encouraged each other and regularly attended Orange Grove together in 1996. I joined the choir and met some amazing sisters and brothers. I felt a deep sense of community, love, and support. It was bittersweet when I had to leave Durham, a community of love, support, and family. It wasn't easy starting over again, but it seems that starting over has been the story of my life.

After I moved to Charlotte, I drove back to Durham for worship weekly until I began participating in local churches. The first church did not acknowledge me as a licensed preacher and did not offer the same love and support that Orange Grove had shown me. Still, I joined under watch care, but I left at the beginning of 1999. I then joined Friendship Missionary Church with Rev. Dr. Clifford A. Jones as pastor. I began to grow in ministry, but it was overwhelming. I was encouraged to attend seminary, serve the pulpit on Sundays, and participate in Saturday worship. I was also a Barnabas' leader for new members. As a woman in the pulpit, I gained a deeper understanding of traditional Black Baptist churches.

Clergywomen wore robes, skirts, dresses, and lap scarves. I didn't understand why I needed a lap scarf or why my suit jacket had to cover my buttocks. The rules reminded me of those that governed my attire in the NOI and elementary school, where I had to be protected from head to toe to prevent men's sexual temptation. I also struggled with writing sermons. I'm a tech person, and English wasn't my strength. Before we preached, the senior pastor always read our sermons to provide feedback. The pastor's feedback on my sermons wasn't pleasant. As a person who performed highly in the tech field, my sermons' feedback was hard to accept. I felt criticized because my English and theological thoughts weren't assimilated. I started drifting away from the church. I welcomed the weekly travel for my job as a consultant. I missed worship and study often. Rarely did anyone from church check in on me to see how things were going or just to say hello we missed you. This was a difficult period as I lived in a new city with no family and new friends.

It's difficult being bi-vocational no matter the career. I was expected to know things about Christianity, but I had to learn the hard way. Seminary wasn't a place to learn about Jesus Christ. My foundation in prayer and study from Orange Grove prepared me theologically. Although I knew the technological world, the black church remained a mystery.

In 2001, I transferred my membership to First Baptist Church West (FBCW), where Rev. Dr. Ricky A. Woods was pastor. I flourished and grew at FBCW. I applied and was accepted to attend The Samuel DeWitt Proctor School of Theology at Virginia Union University. For three years, I drove to Richmond, Virginia. I attended classes on Fridays and Saturdays while working full time at IBM. At FBCW, I was the first woman to serve the pulpit fully. When I started seminary, I didn't have any thoughts of pastoring. I settled for Christian Education.

During my second and third years of seminary, I discovered the church's glass ceiling as a clergywoman and associate minister. Usually, as an associate minister, one preaches only a few times a year. I preached just as much as the youth minister. I served as Minister of Assimilation, women's ministry advisor and support tech as needed. Although women outnumbered men in seminary and church, however men outnumbered women as pastors. Most of the women like me were unpaid associate ministers using our outside gifts and skills in ministry. There were days I worked as many hours in the church as I did for IBM. I worked late nights, made a good impression, and followed all the rules.

In 2002, I commuted weekly to New York City. I informed the project manager that on Fridays, I attended class. Therefore, I would fly back to North Carolina on Thursday nights. The test manager wasn't aware of the arrangement and caused me grief. She was a black woman, and we constantly bumped heads about my Friday night classes. About a month later, we had a come-to-Jesus meeting. I was not silent. I advocated for myself. I wasn't sure what to expect, but it all worked out. She recognized my work and how I managed to balance grad school and IBM work. In the midst of it all, I found a 10-million-dollar issue. From that day forward, the test manager taught me all that she knew and would check my availability to be on her project. Today, we are very close friends.

In 2003, I celebrated my senior year in seminary and my seventh year with IBM. I received an assignment in Cary, North Carolina, which put me 2.5 hours closer to Richmond for class on Friday nights. There were some promises to support my travel that never manifested. For my new assignment, I drove from Charlotte to Cary. I stayed in a hotel or slept on a friend's sofa. I tried to stretch my dollars with household bills, student loans, current educational expenses and housing for the new project. I decided to speak to my manager about my living expenses. When I brought the issue to my manager, who happened to be a woman, she said, "If you don't like it, just quit and leave." I lost all respect for her. I received my lowest performance appraisal ever during this year. As a woman, especially a woman of color I thought she would have my back and fight for travel and living expenses, but she didn't. She made me feel as though I shouldn't have asked for any assistance and struggle to stay employed. Since I could do the assignment from home, I took a hard stance and stayed home until it was time to train my replacement in person.

When I received a low-performance score despite all my hard work, I stopped talking to that manager, and my career stalled for three additional years. Whenever I wanted to move into a different department, resistance hit me in the face. I decided to work on my Master of Science degree in Information Systems. According to my manager, IBM refused to pay my tuition since my studies were not directly related to my work at IBM. Still, I pressed on despite my manager's lack of support and leadership. I received two master's degrees and incurred additional student loan debt. By the time my management structure changed, I had to navigate uncharted territory alone.

Ironically in 2008, another transition occurred. I sensed the call to pastoral leadership. When I inquired about interim pastoral positions, I was made aware retired pastors were filling those positions. There was no support to push my ministry resume forward. I was told to consider chaplaincy in the women's prisons or the hospital because these roles were suitable for women leaders.

In the meantime, I supported a sister in ministry and helped her navigate her way in the ministry. She was a dear friend, and I had no reason not to trust her. Eventually, she stabbed me in the back, making it unbearable for me to serve in my position. My work was undermined, and my friends informed me of her intentions to reveal personal matters. When I was made aware, and without successful arbitration, I left the place I loved, hurt and wounded.

I prided myself on high performance, being detailed-oriented and the go-to person. When women work together, secure and mature in their capabilities, we will support one another. During this period, I learned that I was working with resilient and non-resilient women. As a resilient woman,I knew that I wouldn't keep staying in situations where I would be emotionally and mentally abused.

I almost left IBM because I didn't feel supported. I did leave FBCW because I no longer felt supported. The glass ceiling for women isn't easily broken. As I navigated through these spaces, I realized I would have to struggle continuously with women and men as a woman leader called by God. I'm an ordained Baptist clergywoman with gifts in technology and theology to be used in any church. I thought that changing denominations would make things better. That wasn't the case.

In 2012, I was appointed pastor of St. Paul United Methodist Church, and I was working remotely for IBM. I was the fourth woman to lead the congregation. I moved into the church parsonage because I did not know I had a choice in the matter. I brought my skills, education and life experiences to my first pastorate. At the end of my first year, I had gallbladder surgery. I had a new IBM manager who knew of my complications. When I informed the church, the only concern was making sure the utility bill was paid. The leaders made me feel as if they couldn't trust me. I balanced two households. After I healed from surgery,

I went back to the parsonage. Just a few months later, I became ill again due to mold in the parsonage. I had to move from the parsonage back to my home until the issue was resolved.

One of the men in the congregation said, "We could put you up somewhere while the remediation is being done." I said, "I have a home in Charlotte, and I need a high-speed internet for my full-time job." The third time was the charm after I was able to move back into the parsonage. I was hit with a $600 utility bill because the HVAC had several major issues. I informed my leadership team, which did not offer any support or alternative solutions for paying the utility bill. I had to figure it out on my own. I made up my mind and moved out of the parsonage returned to Charlotte. As a part-time pastor, I drove up for meetings, studies, special events and worship. I struggled in this congregation, and it was even worst when I was cussed out and called evil for not allowing a presentation to happen during worship.

I tell this story because the leadership team was made up of women and men, who did not fully support me with the issues I faced. Instead, some allowed my name to be dragged through the mud. Since many people didn't know me well, I sat in places and overheard what was said about my leadership. It was very hurtful to know a congregation I loved and a denomination I tried to fit in rejected me as a leader. I kept hearing we affirm your gifts, but you are not ready.

In 2016, I was diagnosed with breast cancer. I decided not to share the information with the congregation because of the behavior in 2012 when I had gallbladder surgery. My close friends and those I worked with knew. I didn't understand why I developed breast cancer because no one in my family had it. I tell this story because I felt powerless. My doctor told me it was Stage 0, and all would be well. Actually, I had Stage 2B cancer. The scar tissue from the surgery as a toddler trapped the rest of cancer. I took short-term disability from IBM and time away from the church. After surgery, I became depressed and didn't know why. I'd never been out of work for any long period of time. I felt I had to get back on my feet quickly. I had thought as a leader; I couldn't afford to be out of commission. I had to be there for everyone and put myself on the back burner. I had to be Super Lettie and Super Willetta.

I didn't realize all the unresolved trauma, the hierarchy, patriarchy, misogyny, gender and racial discrimination all weighed heavy on my shoulders because breast cancer made me sit down, and I became angry. In the sit-down period, I needed help to unpack why I felt I needed to rush back to my overwhelming life. I didn't invest in my mental wellness much, but I took a chance and walked through the Sanctuary Counseling Group doors. The first two years were rocky, but I learned so much about myself, especially my coping mechanism. In the last few years, my counselor and I worked on the message that you must prove yourself before you can move forward. I struggled with proving to be a leader. My biggest challenge came from the church and some women on my job. I felt like that little girl who was told, "no, you can't have those drumsticks and pads" again. I was trying to prove I belong, and I was good enough. I couldn't see my giftedness that others saw. All I saw, I needed to do more and be better.

In the push to prove my leadership skills, I unleashed my technical skills in the church and nurtured my leadership skills. It was 2018; I felt a release. I realized I had been holding myself back from being all that God had called me to be. The rewiring of those old messages pushed me from being silent and invisible. I dealt with a lot being bi-vocational. That's another story to tell. I learned a lot in the process, especially pivoting and skipping gears.

Therefore, in November 2019, I had enough of the racism, patriarchy, hierarchy, backstabbing and the lack of support. I found my voice, recognized my purpose and spoke up. I sent a letter to the Bishop, the District Superintendent and others stating my decision not to be reappointed. I shared this information with my church leadership team in confidence, but it was revealed within days to congregation from one of the leaders.

I learned from this experience that confidentiality matters. A leader must be trustworthy and confidential. I was always taught, "your word is your bond." I'm grateful I learned additional leadership skills in the church and the denomination. I strengthen my listening, advocating, negotiating, mentoring, redirecting and nurturing abilities. Although the letter was sent before COVID-19 restrictions, my last day at St. Paul

United Methodist Church remained June 30, 2020, in the middle of a pandemic season. In the eight years as a pastor, they were technologically prepared for a time like this. We moved to virtual Bible Study and then virtual worship during inclement weather during my first few years as pastor.

Today, I recognize I am a gift from my ancestors. As I reflected on what God has for me to do during COVID and leaving the physical pulpit, I also think about my continued healing. My IBM career continues to thrive as I learn to be a more robust and more effective leader, supporter of other women and a mentor to women and men who struggle to find their voice.

Benediction

Now you know my backstory, my pain and my struggles. I'm a late bloomer full of energy. I'm still on the journey as a woman leader. I'm blazing trails and shattering ceilings as much as I can. I wanted to shed some light on places that have been dark far too long. As women lead, some women and men do not see our value. They will devalue women leaders by calling them overly sensitive, insecure and incompetent. They will use phrases like you need a man to do that or you're not qualified. In some roles, women have been bullied by other women and men. The intimidation and traditional patriarchy are used to keep women in their place. Many women don't recognize how they continue patriarchal and misogynistic values in business and the church.

We live in a patriarchal and misogynistic world that sees women as a second-class citizen. We are only important when we behave according to patriarchal values. Through the lenses of patriarchy, gender is assigned as weak or strong based on physical appearance. The world has a lot of systems in place to keep women out of male-dominated roles. Those systems also include caste, colorism, racism, ageism, colonization and gender identification. My family is majority women, and we had to learn to be independent to take care of our families. For my family, this meant we went into fields that provided security, but we had to be emotionally strong and unwavering. Honestly, some women made it more unbearable when working in men-dominated fields; they became trailblazers. Instead of showing how to navigate a new role, they allowed other women to struggle. As you read my back story, I gravitate towards men more than women. They've been more supportive and encouraging in technology and theology.

Therefore today, women have stepped into roles as construction workers, military leaders, electricians, plumbers, CEOs, senior pastors, bishops, presidents, prime ministers, vice presidents and more. I'm thankful for the women and men who nurtured, supported and guided me on this journey. The journey continues for all of us. It's time for us to dismantle sexism, gender inequality, racism, classism, patriarchy and misogyny.

Women leaders are shattering stained glass ceilings and redefining how to lead in male-dominated spaces. Let us lead with authenticity. Traditional gender roles don't work for all women. There's a lot of work to be done. Stacey Abrams of Georgia showed us how to navigate injustice and discrimination towards women from the outside. I realized the traditional woman role didn't work for me. I was wired and set aside for technology, theology and spirituality.

As leaders, both women and men, we have a decision to support women in leadership so that future generations of women leaders will know that they don't have to struggle to be who they have been called to be. It starts with each of us, women, girls, men and boys. My prayer is that we, as women, will encourage our daughters, granddaughters and all girls to know their voices matter and they matter in this world as change agents. We ought to be willing to support one another. If we are unwilling to show respect to one another, then the world will do the same. My continued prayer for this book to raise awareness of womens' struggle in life, leadership, education and other areas. Moreover, women in the workplace do not have to be at odds with each other. We all are gifted, and there's plenty of room on the ladder and through the shattered glass ceilings where we were once restricted. I leave you with two parking lot discussions and encourage you to start a book club. My story is one of many stories. Every woman has a story to tell that goes back several generations or just one. I finally found the courage to tell my story now. Instead of immediately saying "No," to a women's dream, open the door to her "Yes." For my brothers, let's be more than an ally to the women in your lives. Let us walk together, support one another and encourage one another. This is just one way we can dismantle the glass ceiling together.

During this book's writing, the 46th President of the United States of America was elected by the people. With this historic election, it is the first time in the United States of America's history that a woman of African and Asian descent, a graduate of a Historically Black College and University and a member of the oldest black sorority will fill the second in command position as Vice President-elect. Senator Kamala Harris' mother is from India, and her father is from Jamaica. As a woman, she will face challenges because most of the country will expect her and the First Lady-elect Dr. Jill Biden to assume the traditional women's role. When we succumb to others' opinions on how we should behave in certain roles, we will rob ourselves of our authentic self.

One last thing, this year, 2020, the United States celebrated the 100th year of the 19th Amendment. The women in the United States of America received the right to vote. However, black women and women of color could not exercise that right until the Voting Rights Act of 1965. Let's not wait another 100 years or 55 years to make a change. Change is right before our eyes.

Amen, Amen and Amen!

Parking Lot Discussion 1
Questions to Ponder

☙ Looking back on your life, are you able to see how you were uniquely created?

☙ What can you do to help girls and women feel they belong?

☙ What do you need to feel so that your voice is heard and your presence is seen?

☙ Where can you make the best impact to help others through their struggle?

☙ If you weren't told NO, where would you be today?

☙ If you are a woman leader, do you have a diverse group of potential women in your circle?

☙ If you struggled in a male-dominated role, what strategies have been put into place so that other women won't struggle?

☙ There are times we appear to be difficult to work with. Where does that perception come from?

☙ Who sees you as a role model?

☙ What are some things you can do to dismantle policies and practices that discriminate against all women?

Parking Lot Discussion 2
Myths to Dismantle

Myth 1 - Girls and Women are too bossy, sensitive, and passive to be leaders.

Myth 2 - Girls and women must take responsibility for dressing in a nonsexual manner without showing body parts.

Myth 3 - Only boys can play the drums.

Myth 4 - Girls are not interested in electronics & technology.

Myth 5 - Dreams die when children arrive.

Myth 6 - Deferred dreams disappear for good.

Myth 7 - Black girls and women can't encourage each other.

Myth 8 - Nobody will pull you to the side and talk with you.

Myth 9 - Women are not supportive of other women.

Myth 10 - Women ought to be grateful for whatever they receive.

About the Author

The Reverend Willetta "Lettie" Ar-Rahmaan, a bi-vocational ordained Baptist Minister, a Senior I/T Specialist at IBM, the Visionary of On The Move Ministries, LLC and a board member of the Wesley Community Development Corporation, and a council member of the Wesleyan Contemplative Order.

Rev. Lettie holds an Associate of Science in Data Processing from Gateway Community College A Bachelor of Science in Computer Science with a minor in Business Administration from North Carolina Central University, a Master of Science in Information Systems from Strayer University, and a Master of Divinity from The Samuel DeWitt Proctor School of Theology at Virginia Union University.

She received a Technology All-Star Award for Women of Color in STEM, designed and self-published two devotional/prayer journals, "Dancing with God" and "Lord Take My Ordinary Life and Mind," for women's ministries. Her sermon "Breaking the Silence" was published in The African American Pulpit Spring of 2007 journal.

Lettie is a teenage sexual abuse survivor and a breast cancer thriver. Her tag line #educatehealprevent. She believes that we can help people heal, promote awareness and prevention through education.

Connect with Lettie below:

Instagram: @revlettiea
LinkedIn: @willettaa

www.ingramcontent.com/pod-product-compliance
Lightning Source LLC
Chambersburg PA
CBHW051336120626
46547CB00016B/2560